THE PRESS'S ROLE
IN BAD POLITICS
What They Do &
How They Contribute

Table of Contents

No table of contents entries found.

Pride and Prejudice

I'm going to lump the press into the same category as big business because they walk the walk and talk the talk. Ergo they are indeed big business. In stark contrast to my personal opinion, reporters might imagine themselves as being...
-- independent members of the fourth estate (*a coined phrase by Edmund Burke during a parliamentary debate in 1792 on the opening up of press reporting in the House of Commons in England*)
-- guardians against government evils
-- purveyors of the truth

In reality their reporting more often finds them in the categories of both government collaborators and show business outlets. By this I mean that their performance is often directed at facilitating political deceit and pandering to sensationalism, as much as it is toward probing for and providing pertinent news.

During the 2008 Presidential campaign, one of the talking heads at a round table discussion conceded that he and his fellow reporters were responsible for creating the candidates momentum or loss of the same. This was acknowledged while displaying a look of pride. Interestingly there was no objection from the other journalists at this affair. So it is clear that they know the bitter truth about their manipulation of the public, and they do not much care to correct it.

It is reasonable to assume that one of the presses' primary roles should be to ask probing questions to reveal the truth and expose dishonesty. Personal biases ought to be left at home and not be incorporated into the coloring of their reporting. Far too often this is wishful thinking. Let me demonstrate common press biases by first analyzing the appropriate technique for interrogating a witness in our courts...
-- unless the judge permits a lawyer to treat a defendant as hostile, statements that are accusatory may not be allowed
-- questions may not begin with a leading or assumption-directed phrases like: "Isn't it true that..."or "Didn't you..."
-- rather the phrasing must be: "Is it true that..." or "Did you..."

These rules of conduct should similarly be used by members of the press as a proper method for keeping their agendas out of the questioning. However, it is not unusual to have reporters express their personal beliefs couched in their queries because there is no one to stop them... certainly not their bosses who must encourage that behavior. Attitude peddling puts the press in the position of making or tainting the news, rather than just reporting on it. One motivation behind the presses' methods of questioning can be explained as a tawdry effort to interject sensationalism into the reporting process because this is what viewers/readers want. As a result, we get what we ask for. An unbiased press is a nice theory, but it is not the norm. To demonstrate this absence of straight forward reporting we might ask ourselves....

-- Do the media outlets have an obvious preponderance of liberal or conservative columnists on their staffs?

-- Are their news stories slanted in a particular direction without an accurate representation of both sides of each issue?

-- Do they voice expressed or implied support for one candidate or issue over another?

-- Do the reporters ask leading, rather than probing questions?

-- Are they inclined to be neutral?

Presses' Inclinations

One of the proclivities of the press is to report on an event or topic using the term <u>reportedly</u> in order to attach a hint of veracity to a news story. What exactly does reportedly mean? It may mean that someone wishes to remain anonymous, and passes along confidential information to a reporter. However, this in no way implies that the disclosed "facts" have veracity. It may be the quoted person's method of poisoning the waters of an opponent. Or it may be used to deflect attention from an issue. Far too often the press uses this ruse to get newsprint or air time.

In point of fact, the press is less exacting with the truth than are most of us. After all they are paid by the word and not necessarily by a thought's merits or its authenticity. Why do you think the press drones on endlessly over stories that deserve little more than a passing glance? Did we really need…
-- six days of news about President Ford's funeral
-- the months of bylines regarding a college sex scandal
-- the endless rant about the death of a wife by her playboy husband
-- an obsession with the Congressperson who groped his staff members
-- focusing on Congressperson's who cheat on their mates (*which is immoral*) rather than their voting records (*which can also be immoral*).

And don't think that the anniversary of each traumatic event from recent history will escape there attention either. Nothing much has changed with Charles Manson in a quarter of a century, but he still hits the news on an annual basis. Where would the press be without a tickler file?

The press can be so preoccupied with the specter of tasteless sensationalism because there is a ready audience for this kind of foolishness, which is sometimes called yellow journalism. No horrific story is allowed to go under-reported. One of the channels in my area goes so far as to dedicate most of their evening news budget to as many police blotter stories (*murder, rape, pedophiles, hit and run*) as they can locate. Do we really learn anything valuable from this type of reporting? It certainly does not uncover what our politicians have failed to accomplish while they are in office due to their conflicted money-raising activities. But that disclosure would require real reporting which is not in most reporters' playbooks.

Mark Twain, author: *If you don't read the newspaper you are uninformed, if you do read the newspaper you are misinformed.*

News by Assassination

Now that cable television has become a major medium for the dissemination of news, we are inundated with the talking heads who both create and exploit controversy. They may express personal and occasionally vitriolic opinions, perhaps more than they present news. They drone on endlessly with tawdry attitudes that fill the airwaves and use tortured logic in an effort to make political hay for their favored issue, party or candidate. Because of this failure to be impartial, we should ask...

-- How dare reporters and networks align themselves into liberal and conservative camps anyway?

-- Is that the best way to present the news and inform the public?

-- Can't we find people with a balanced point of view and no political ax to grind?

-- Shouldn't we insist on honesty and integrity from the news corporations?

On both the ultra-conservative and ultra-liberal sides of the spectrum we have a string of commentators (*notice that I did not say reporters*) who seem to relish the limelight that they have created for themselves. Why else would they be invited to visit the late night variety shows if they weren't in show business? And this celebrity is accomplished at the expense of unbiased reporting. While a few may make an effort to present the news in a relatively impartial fashion, the majority are preoccupied with casting aspersions on their targets as often as they

can manage. Forget that this contrived melodrama takes the format of…
-- innuendo
-- exaggeration
-- distortion
-- out of context quotes (*especially*)
-- deliberate misinterpretation
-- outright lies

I guess the current king of deliberate misrepresentation is Sean Hannity on the Fox channel, only because I do not listen to the radio talk shows, which must surely be in the running for this dubious honor. His biases can be so blatant and irrational that they have become annoying to listen to, which is a long way from being informative. Essentially he has cast himself as a rabble rouser with only a passing concern for the truth. Often that infrequent truth is couched among half-truths and lies.

Corporations that employ these personalities do so, not for the straightforward presentation of news and the accuracy of statements, but for the ratings that they crave. Audiences will believe almost anything if it is presented with enough conviction, emotion, authority and repetition… including after an incidence has been debunked by legitimate authority.

In years gone by the three major network anchors appeared to disseminate a relatively dispassionate view of the daily news. In fact as a child I wished for presentations to be a bit more revealing or controversial, especially when it came to news about the politicians. But in a classic case of be careful what you wish for, that tide has turned. Much of cable programming that passes for news has an entertainment quality, and occasionally nasty quotient to it.

In 2013 Obama gave his State of the Union address. This was followed by the Republican reply, as has become usual. Marko Rubio was tapped as the up-and-comer in the ranks to deliver the opposition's message. During his speech he leaned awkwardly to retrieve a bottle of water and take a sip. No big deal, right? Wrong. The in-Obama's-pocket media turned it into a mini-indictment of Marko for the uncomfortable movement. So when the liberal press wants to degrade someone, they will not hesitate to pick on anything that they can get away with.

The social reporting on celebrities is even worst. Do we really need to care about the out-of-control lives of these pampered, self-centered brats? A case in point about slanted coverage would be the initial fifteen minute apology of Tiger Woods regarding his extra-marital affairs. While my wife and I thought that his contrition was reasonably on point, members of the blather media generally gave him poor marks for reading a prepared speech and for not taking any question. Like little children who wanted to play with someone else's toy, they felt that Tiger selfishly took control of the event. It did not matter that he responded to questions on the minds of most people. He was berated by these media for not giving them their fair share of time. Could that criticism be any more revealing of how they see themselves as being entitled? Talk about arrogance!

In the ninety days prior Tiger's TV appearance, the celebrity press was involved in hundreds, perhaps thousands of hours devoted to dissecting his personality, personal life, and illicit behavior. Their opinions were not labeled as such, but they were presented as insights by those in the know. The truth is that these commentators demonstrated virtually nothing beyond wild guesses, assumptions, and fabrications.

In an interesting addendum to the above, the press saw fit to interview at least one of the women who were involved in the affairs with Tiger. The person that I saw being given her fifteen minutes of shame lamented the fact that Tiger did not apologize to her since he had said that he loved her. Could this person possibly be even more self-absorbed than Tiger? He was married, you know. How does she figure that her rights were abridged? Did she ever think about the rights of Tiger's wife? Sounds like a sleazy bar-broad to me.

Creating the Issues

Rarely does the national TV press ignore an opportunity to criticize a candidate for changing their mind on a major issue… <u>flip-flopping</u> as they are inclined to call it. We should all appreciate that life and circumstances are constantly in a state of flux, and that only the most stubborn person would not be willing to learn a new lesson when the opportunity comes along. Yet the incident-creation types that wield the airwaves would have us believe that taking a new stance more often than once in a blue moon indicates a lack of integrity. According to the press, if we can not believe what is said on some date forever, than how could we ever believe any other things that the candidate has said? This is either…
-- a fool's logic
-- a shallow effort to impugn someone's veracity without real justification
-- a shameless attitude that makes for good press

At a political rally in 2007 John McCain made a modest joke by paraphrasing the Beach Boys' song Barbara Ann. He devilishly changed a refrain to <u>bomb Iran</u>. It was more interesting than funny, but the press invented a seamy side to the lyrics and tried to make an issue of it. McCain's appropriate and quick response was that they "lighten up and get a life". It was nice to see someone refuse to back down to the sensation seekers that have found a home in the press corps. That episode demonstrates how desperate some reporters are to get their fifteen seconds of air time or protect their job security.

I can imagine that the newspaper's daily editor/reporter meetings are not only filled with intellectual talk about which of the stories are more important than others, or which deserve the front page of the paper, or first position on the TV news broadcast. They must also discuss how to sensationalize them for the public appetite because that is what people want. If this were not true, there would not be dozens of pages and hours of television devoted to the latest campus shooting or a missing child. How does a campus shooting differ from the hundreds of other shootings that may occur daily? The answer is wealthy, white-collar offspring. When we may want legitimate sensationalism, the press is mostly mute. For example, we know little beyond the daily body count of what is happening in Iraq and Afghanistan, which are government controlled news venues. There is seldom a mention of how much those countries' people may be suffering or (*especially*) why they blame Americans for much of that sorrow. After all, we need to be viewed by ourselves as the good guys. And the press corps has no incentive to upset that particular applecart because they feed off it.

To get into the reasons why Arabs may blame us for their difficulties, we have to try to understand their mindset. They...
-- are religious in the extreme
-- do not co-exist well with other religions
-- label non-Arabs as infidels
-- believe that their homeland is only their land

-- will not tolerate "invaders" (*everyone else*)
-- would rather live under religious tyranny than under democratic "oppression" because this is their culture
-- dismiss freedom as a political con that is played on the Europeans and Americans
-- might rather be blown up than submit to Western ideas
-- believe that an honorable death is to be revered and not feared
think we are too stupid to go home (*ok, on this last point they have my full agreement*)

Does any of the above make sense to you? These arguments against staying the Middle East do not seem to sway more than a handful of our politicians.

Press Promotions

The press is also not with out guilt in manufacturing those false heroes which we may have come to admire. For example, when a President dies, the only people who are asked to bear witness about his presidency and persona to the media are the deceased's friends and well-wishers. Had I not been aware of Presidential behaviors that frequently have been dishonorable, I might be moved by this contrived adulation. It is not my intention to personally denigrate Gerald Ford and George Bush… just note that they were under-qualified office holders. Likable or not, the job of being President was substantially over their heads, as Gerry once conceded. And Ford performed a thoughtless disservice to the country when he preemptively pardoned Richard "I am not a crook" Nixon, the de facto leader of the Watergate felons. Lately the wags are giving Ford high marks for this intervention in the justice process as responsible for putting that unfortunate event behind us. So with this logic, should we let all felons out of prison because it degrades our image?

Even today President Nixon, the preeminent poster boy for *corrupt government starts at the top* is now being forgiven by the press for his…
-- enemies list
-- paranoia
-- shady dealings
-- direct association with felons
-- being an un-indicted conspirator

Press Passivity

We apparently have short memories when it comes to recalling the negative aspects of our political history as they relate to our Presidents. Or perhaps we just can't stand to think of them as the felons that they occasionally are. Do you remember when President Johnson had that juicy broadcast license for an Austin radio station delivered to his wife Lady Bird in spite of intense competition for the plum? Did the press have more than a passing reference or two to this event?

Prior to Nixon's journey into infamy, his aids were putting out feelers about having him nominated for a Nobel Peace Prize. This was ostensibly justified by his ending the Viet Nam war and ordering our troops home. So the act of stopping a previous, illegitimate policy of President Johnson was purported to make a world hero out of Nixon. Does anyone wonder just how Nixon's aids thought that they might be successful with their Peace Prize promotion? And aren't you just a little bit curious about what putting out feelers implies? Perhaps it means that they thought the Nobel committee could be manipulated in some way. Or a darker explanation might be that the mere mention of Nixon and Nobel in the same breath would enhance his image for the next election.

Does all of this slight of hand mean that we have not had a number of respect-worthy Presidents? No. But perhaps there were more in our early history rather than later years. While some of our recent

Presidents may have performed well at their duties, that fact does not imply that there weren't a number of their peers who might have executed that job just as competently or better. It also does not necessarily follow that our most-revered Presidents had carried out their duties all that well in spite of press reporting to the contrary. Americans just like to have our heroes regardless of whether or not it makes sense and is accurate. It is all part of the Indian and chief genetics that sanctions our respect for leaders even though it is out sync with their abilities or integrity.

Because of our gullibility, government officials can and do lie to us with impunity, then suffer little exposure from that charade

Who is in Charge?

Subsequent to the lawsuit that was filed by Dan Rather against CBS in 2007, it became evident that the press's practice of corrupt reporting goes well beyond its reporters. If one can put faith in Dan's contention about CBS management, the executives that own the news outlets are also responsible for misshaping the news. Their pressure to suppress or slant stories amounts to censorship, just as leaving out details or ignoring obvious conclusions would. Dan related that the documents which would have condemned Bush's unmilitary-like military record, and the opportune loss of same, had not been conclusively demonstrated to be either accurate or inaccurate. They were just conveniently missing. Yet CBS was alleged to have forced Dan into an on-air apology to maintain good relations with the White

House. So one has to ask, do we really want news outlets cultivating cozy relations with the same government entities that they are supposed to be reporting on? Do we want the chickens hanging out in the foxes den and doing their bidding?

The Presses' Role

The epidemic-level of political malfeasance that is part and parcel of public office is made possible thanks to (*ta da*) the average folks who want to believe the best about their elected officials, and who seldom question what mischief they may be up to. This applies equally to the press because they can occasionally be up to no good as well. For example, they are less than critical of the...
-- political press handouts which may be accepted as gospel
-- politician's statements that are generally taken at face value
-- evasive answers that are allowed to go unchallenged
-- taxpayer-paid, press-tag-along trips with Presidents that go lightly reported
-- shameful "debate" that goes on in Congress

Another aspect of the under-reported behavior that takes place while in office is the sense of entitlement demonstrated by elected officials. Take Barak Obama for example. Those who are fortunate enough to travel with the President on mind-numbingly-expensive jaunts around the globe are seldom critical of the cost, even though they should be fully aware of it. The perk is just too much to pass up in spite of the manipulation effect is has on reporters.

Another White House directed exploitation is Washington's elite reporters being invited to party at cozy "press events" with the same officials they may be assigned to report on. And of course they want to be invited back for the next up-close-and-personal gala by limiting their aggressive reporting. This is not exactly the arm's length arrangement that the forth estate should have establish for themselves. Rarely has there been a President like Obama who pushed so many controversial issues that were against the will of the electorate. Being surrounded by yes-persons 24/7 and encountering minimal, in-depth press coverage may be the factors in developing this self-serving attitude.

The difference between reporters and automobile salespeople is that we all know that the later are deceitful

Yes, the press does provide a few stories that may expose some of the questionable behaviors of politicians, but this is usually done without crossing the line of press etiquette. When these disclosures do occur, reporters may be exposing just the tip of the iceberg with their limited follow-up. Or they may be mostly picking on those whose behaviors are over the top. If the press corps were only marginally aggressive in their corruption reporting they could fill the news with political activity for which you and I might go to jail.

In 2009 New Jersey sting operation, the feds netted dozens of high ranking officials, including some Mayors, who were indicted for corruption. Yet until the feds revealed these arrests, the dealings of this band of alleged felons were virtually unknown to the public. If you can have this many persons involved in a conspiracy to subvert government, it should not have been a complete secret. After all how did the feds conclude that something was wrong if there was no smoke around this fire? So where was the press when the conspiracy was going down?

Another of the press's gifts that are bestowed on politicians is allowing a lack of attribution by the government's rules-makers to their pronouncements and dictates. There is hardly a day that goes by without a press story assigning credit to some nameless, faceless, element, such as...
-- the Pentagon said this
-- the VA refused to do that
-- the State Department did this...
-- the Justice Department decided not to pursue...

Well who exactly are there anonymous people any way? I am fairly sure that the government buildings do not make our public policy. Because we rarely learn the names of the persons that are responsible for our government's actions, those who are making the decisions are conveniently protected by this veil of secrecy. Others who are in a position to know the inside story may have their own jobs to protect. Consequently they may be disinclined to risk any retribution with an ill-advised revelation. The result of this secrecy is that the bureaucrats are relatively free to set policies and practices that may be in conflict with the public good.

Do you remember when the press dutifully reported those trumped-up stories about the remains of Iraqi chemical factories being discovered in dilapidated tractor trailers for example? Right! Our countries' chemical factories occupy hundreds of acres, but those clever, sandal-footed Iraqis were so sophisticated that they could produce nerve gases in dirty, non-air-conditioned truck trailers in the middle of the desert. The shallow thinkers in our press initially bought this fabrication. Then there was VP Cheney's subsequent role in the manufactured WMD stories which his office blamed on other agencies for an information failure. Had the press corp and Congress been more diligent (*say at the sixth grade level*) we wouldn't be killing Americans in a country that wants no part of us and has so little regard for their own lives.

This current militaristic attitude may have been encouraged by the memberships of Bush, Cheney, Rice and Rhumsfeld in The Project for the New American Century, a non-profit, "educational" organization dedicated to a few fundamental propositions. Among their platforms are the beliefs that...
-- American leadership is good for both America and for the world
-- such leadership requires military strength, diplomatic energy and commitment to moral principle
-- we should rally support for a vigorous and principled policy of American international involvement

Now that the truth about the war had somewhat come to light, is it any wonder why Cheney chose not to test the political waters, much less run for President? Oh yes, and what became of the expose' of his previous company, Halliburton, and their misappropriation of hundreds of millions of dollars from the war's reconstruction effort. And why were fees still being paid to them to help restore Iraq? Where was there the press follow-up on this alleged theft of taxpayer money?

When there is no press accountability of officials, there is corruption

Press and Context

What may arguably be the worst case of the press's penchant for ruthlessly taking people's words and intent out of context is the controversy that erupted in 2008 regarding Reverend Wright and Barak Obama. Because Wright had expressed his frustration with the establishment in excessive terms, he was derided by the press in a most uncharitable manner. There is little doubt this was only because Barak was a parishioner in the Reverend's church, and would not have received any attention otherwise. While I do not understand Wright's rant about the government creating aids to control blacks and other odd statements, I judged his "God damn America" refrain to mean *God damn the government for not making America color blind*. You may not like the words he chose, but it would be hard to argue with the intent behind them, if I got it right.

Wright's later speech before the NAACP, however, could not have been more inspiring. Perhaps it was the speech of the decade regarding race relations, but one that will surely be ignored for years. His argument was that Blacks being different is not the same thing as Blacks being deficient, referring to the way in which African Americans are sometimes cast because of their local speech patterns. He went on to say that we are all different in a variety of ways and no one should be labeled as inferior because of that. I would challenge anyone to read his speech and come away without having that understanding reinforced.

But the ever vigilant press jumped at the opportunity to repeatedly broadcast a few maliciously chosen, out of context phrases with which to condemn him. They apparently could not resist their prime directive to indulge in trivialization and sensationalism whenever possible. Wright's examples of discrimination against Blacks was to repeat two well known Presidential quotes in his poorly attempted accents of Kennedy and Johnson. He went on to point out that they had not been demeaned for communicating in their regional tongues. But when Blacks converse in their dialect they are put down as inferior. So how did the press present this to the public? Almost unbelievably they extracted the two phrases in such a way as to portray Wright as mocking Kennedy and Johnson, which by anyone's reading was not his intention. Then armed with their distorted reporting, they went on to disparage Wright as a vindictive person and someone who may have been out to damage Obama. Talk about creating news from nonsense! I have no evidence to show that the press was attempting to do Obama a favor by allowing him to further distance himself from Wright, but they certainly maligned Wright for some reason. Maybe it was just another case of creating fodder for the sensationalism-hungry public.

More Good ol' Boys

Political appointments are a necessary evil of our system of government. There are so many positions to fill that someone has to do that job. The general public clearly has insufficient knowledge of who is qualified and who is not, as witnessed by the candidates that they elect to office. On the other hand, the President and his kiss-up-to-keep-my-job advisors are in only a slightly better position to make these judgments. As a result, those who offer up loyalty, money, or favors to advance an administration are likely to benefit (*no surprise*) from their "unselfish" service. Of course this behavior is not limited to the top levels of government. Rather it is endemic to government in general.

We have gotten so used to having politicians working for themselves that we may ignore their questionable campaign financing and overspending proclivities. Congress, in one example, has passed legislation funding the lavish funerals of our Presidents without asking anyone's permission but themselves. Certainly they did not ask those of us who end up with the bill. Weren't these now deceased politicians paid more than enough to bury themselves? In addition to the generous funerals, there is the substantial cost of...
-- military bands
-- rifle corps
-- dozens of funeral cars
-- jets flying overhead
-- thousands of flowers

-- meals and lodging for invited guests (*did you get your invitation?*)

Then we have to pay to fly the departed and their entourage to a final resting place on multiple Air Force 747s. Don't you wish you were part of this fraternity that treats itself so nicely on someone else's dime? No wonder Betty Ford was overheard to whisper "It's beautiful" at Jerry's funeral, as if she had some right to that extravaganza for which she did not offer to pay one red cent. Will you get a decommissioned Air Force One, as Regan did near his Presidential library?

While President's Ford, Regan, and Kennedy funerals were grand productions, who are the benefactors of this showiness? You? I? Likely it is the politicians who may gain a degree of undeserved credibility from the *it rubs off on me* effect of these extravaganzas. If we elevate our Presidents to this monarch-like status, then with an innocent-by-association we tend to also elevate Congresspersons as a group. Perhaps there could be some small benefit to those who are obsessed with the rich and famous.

We should be aware that our leaders have not been, for the most part, particularly virtuous people since it is not even remotely possible in the world of politics. We should not behave as if they were saints after their deaths, because that demonstrates how little attention we pay to their performances during life.

This adulation also tells politicians that what they are doing in office is ok, which is surely not the case.

Part of keeping Presidential images from being as tarnished as their behavior often dictates resides with the incestuous association they enjoy with the press. The press is about as untainted as are the drug companies that offer perks to the doctors in exchange for their prescription business. Anyone attending a White House sponsored press events demonstrates their willingness to indulge in a conflict of interest and discounts their responsibility to the public. But then who do we have to complain to... the press?

My criticism of our Presidents is not meant to demean all of those who have held that position, whether they were bumbling, adequate or enlightened. It is only meant to put their performance into perspective. They and the millions of government workers run the largest company in the world and are certainly due some respect for that effort. What they are not entitled to is...
-- our mostly thoughtless support
-- their overly generous benefits
-- our tendency to treat Presidents like royalty
-- an average of $7.000/year more than we pay for similar work in the private sector

Unjustified respect for people imbues more power on the powerful, makes possible more wealth for the wealthy, and bestows more privilege on the privileged

I have mentioned the delinquency of the press many times and with good justification. They may fancy themselves as watchdogs of government, but it is not difficult to tell that reality and cultivated images are far different. During elections, voters are seldom given the kind of information that could help them make well-informed decisions. Instead they are bombarded with air time from and about candidates that spin the truth, rather then enlighten us. And the press is just as adept at spin as are the politicians. Their op-eds are filled with opinions, attitudes and disparagements that show little regard for facts. Even having their errors brought to light does not stop the prevarication as long as commentators think they can gain an additional mile out of a false statement.

Adding insult to injury, broadcasts are filled with commercials and teasers (*you know... stay tuned for whatever*). We are routinely bombarded with these "coming attractions" that are injected at the end of a news segment to peak our interest and keep us from changing stations. If we want the details about some issue that was mentioned we must endure the commercial delay. And we may have to wait for the second or third segment down the road before the promised information is presented. Occasionally the teaser occupies more time then does that actual data.

American Monarchy

While presidential excesses are by no means limited to Obama, he has set a new benchmark for over the top travel spending. It is not just foreign royalties that fly with a fleet of luxurious jets to far off destinations for a few hours, rather than using the phone to conduct business. Are you aware that his frequent travels include...

-- a second jumbo jet for the press and other VIPs?

-- several planes for the President's many vehicles and staffers

-- airplanes bringing in tanker trucks for the President's planes to guarantee that the fuel is not tampered with

-- contingents of anti-terrorist military located along motorcade routes

-- copious supplies - ranging from lighting, to red carpets, and speaker stands, that are just the tip of equipment-iceberg

-- Michelle Obama taking her hairdresser (*can she no longer comb her own hair?*), along with a large contingent of superfluous staffers, aboard Air Force One trips, with nary a peep from the press

-- vacations to Hawaii that have been reported to cost taxpayers about $1.5 million per week

-- a trip made to Africa to underscore the President's commitment to malaria containment (*I guess the phones were down that day*)

-- in the first weeks of the nuclear problem in Japan, Obama played golf and took his family on a trip to Brazil (*Does that remind anyone of the Bush administration's lack of reaction to Katrina?*)

In the election year of 2012 Obama used the travel resources of the White House to make various trips to "swing" states at the taxpayer's expense. The House Speaker, Boehner, criticized these trips as merely political, which if true must, by federal law, be paid for by Obama's election campaign. One of the trips was said to be nothing more than a "fake fight" with Congress regarding federally funded student loan rates. This criticism, of course, misses the point since the President has the resources of regular press events at which he could easily voice his concerns, either directly or through the White House press office. So we end up paying millions of dollars for his lavish trips which are purely political in nature, and then the President lies (*implicitly*) about their need for the public benefit… obviously without remorse over their costs. The entitled can never spend too much to become embarrassed, apparently.

In 2013 a wildfire devastated the Arizona town of Yarnell and parts of nearby People's Valley. After both Obama and Biden (*who attended the event to honor the 19 killed firefighters*) promised that the government would do all it could to support those in need, FEMA informed the AZ governor that government disaster/emergency funds would not be forthcoming. That same week Obama flew to AZ for a meet and greet event at untold expense. It seems there is plenty of money for his nonsense trips, vacations, and other taxpayer rip-offs (*Congressional pork*), but not enough for the past victims of Katrina or this recent tragedy. While the governor made an issue of this, others were not nearly as outspoken.

So where is the press when all of these taxpayer rip-off are going on? In the second plane, of course.

Knowledge Suppression

Information is occasionally suppressed by the news media, politicians, corporations and government agencies because it is in their interest to do so. This distortion occurs because...
-- the news media is beholding to politicians and agencies who feed them propaganda
-- government agencies are obligated to politicians who fund their money-wasting bureaucracies
-- politicians are indebted to the large corporations who pull the strings with their campaign financing (*bribes*)
-- large corporations are obliged to, well no one actually, because they are truly -the owners of government

These circumstances add up to the incestuous relationships that conspire to suppress meaningful information from being disclosed to the public and beneficial laws from being passed. Perhaps the most infamous of these naked suppressions took place a few years back when Ralph Nader was making a run for President. The press would give disparaging lip service to his candidacy, and then just as often it would misrepresent his views. The press encouraged us to believe that a vote for Ralph was a wasted vote, and that it was tantamount to a vote for the Republicans because most of Nader's supporters would have been inclined to vote Democratic.

The information control went so far as to prevent Nader from joining the Presidential debates in the

2000 election. Third party candidates were alleged to be detrimental to democracy, and were viewed as being a liability to a stable two-party system. Third party candidates are indeed "injurious" to our political system because they foster the presentation of new ideas and may not let politicians hide behind their Coke vs. Pepsi subterfuge (*described elsewhere*).

Not too surprisingly, the debates referred to above were run by officials from the Republican and Democratic national committees, not by the organization that stood in as their stalking horse, the Daughters of the American Revolution (*DAR*). They were used to put an independent face on what was a bipartisan conspiracy. Shame on the DAR for getting its fifteen minutes of fame by being manipulated this ignoble manner! It was quite some time before this critical information was revealed by the press.

When Ralph Nader arrived at one of these debates with a valid ticket for a seat in the audience, the police refused him entry into the auditorium, and threatened him with arrest if he insisted on taking a seat. His picture, and those of the others who were cast as enemies, had been placed in the so-called Book of Faces (*persons who were to be denied admittance*). The politicians and the interests that were behind this restriction of free assembly could not risk a breach in their wall of secrecy which prevents the disclosure of who is truly running this country. Interfering with the controlled, two-party system might uncover that fact to the masses, they correctly reasoned. This *control of process* is only marginally less obnoxious than what occurs in the banana republics that we have vehemently criticized.

Kip's Books & Links

The books listed here are available in ebook format for Kindle™ and Nook™ readers at Amazon.com and elsewhere. Some of the shorter materials are "ideas" booklets or excerpts from longer books. Hard copy books are available at Createspace.com. The URL links, where listed, access book previews.

A BETTER BATHROOM - An Ideas Guide
Construction
https://www.createspace.com/Preview/1134187
$1.99   34 pages

A BETTER KITCHEN - An Ideas Guide
Construction
https://www.createspace.com/Preview/1134190
$1.99   36 pages

AGGRESSION & BULLYING - It's Not Just Our Wiring
Human Nature
$1.49   11 pages

AN OUTDOOR KITCHEN - The Latest Trend?
Construction
$1.49   6 pages

BEFORE STARTING HOME CONSTRUCTION - What You Need To Know In Advance
Construction
https://www.createspace.com/Preview/4136208
$2.99/$5.49   40 pages

BRAIN CHOICES & FREE WILL - Getting To Know Ourselves Using Concepts That Are Not Well Understood Or Accepted
Human Nature
https://www.createspace.com/Preview/1134191
$3.99/$5.99   78 pages

CUSTOM HOME DOs & DON'Ts - The ULTIMATE Guide To Getting Your Custom Home DONE RIGHT!
Construction
https://www.createspace.com/Preview/1134192
$6.99/10.49   266 pages

DECEPTION IN AMERICA - How We Are Manipulated Big Business, Politicians, The Press & Our Indoctrinations
Government/Business/Politics
https://www.createspace.com/Preview/1134195
$9.99/15.99   458 pages

EVOLUTION, THE BRAIN, & RELIGION - How Evolution Made Us What We Are
Human Nature
https://www.createspace.com/Preview/1134196
$4.99/$6.99   160 pages

EXCESSIVE EXECUTIVE COMPENSATION - What You Should Know About The Fleecing Of America By Executives & Boards
Government/Business/Politics
$1.49   11 pages

FOLLOWING THE CROWD - How We Fall In Line With Others
Human Nature
$1.49   14 pages

FUN WITH APPETIZERS - For Those Who Like To Entertain Well
Cookbook
https://www.createspace.com/Preview/4438108
$3.99/$5.99   70 pages

FUN WITH CARBOS - The Cookbook For Those Without A Care
Cookbook

https://www.createspace.com/Preview/4440041
$3.99/$5.99   94 pages

FUN WITH CHICKEN - The Fowl & Seafood Cookbook That
Avoids Red Meat
Cookbook
https://www.createspace.com/Preview/4441007
$4.99/$6.99   148 pages

FUN WITH DESSERTS - The - What To Do When The
Meal Is Over - Cookbook
Cookbook
https://www.createspace.com/Preview/4444531
$2.99/$5,49   64 pages

FUN WITH ENTREES - Getting To The Heart Of Cooking
Cookbook
https://www.createspace.com/Preview/1135491
$5.99/$8.99   172 pages

FUN WITH MEAT - The Carnivore's Cookbook
Cookbook
https://www.createspace.com/Preview/4436803
$3.99/$5.99   110 pages

FUN WITH SALADS - My Take On The Classics & Others
https://www.createspace.com/Preview/1136150
$1.99/$5.49   24 pages

FUN WITH SEAFOOD – See Food & Eat It Cookbook
Cookbook
https://www.createspace.com/Preview/4494327
$3.99/$5.99   84 pages

FUN WITH SOUP - It's Economical, & Healthy As Well
Cookbook
https://www.createspace.com/Preview/4442511
$1.99/$5.49   38 pages

FUN WITH WINE - Aging And Tasting Wine
$1.49   9 pages
An informative guide, including wine-term explanations.

GOVERNMENT FOR PEOPLE? - How the US government "functions" without regard for the negative ramifications of its actions
Government/Business/Politics
https://www.createspace.com/Preview/1134204
$3.99/$5.99   88 pages

HOME DESIGN GOALS - Important Considerations
Construction
https://www.createspace.com/Preview/1134209
$1.99/$5.49   36 pages

HOME GREEN HOME - The Ins & Outs Of Home Efficiency
Construction
https://www.createspace.com/Preview/1134208
$2.99/$5.49   42 pages

HOW BUSINESS FAILS US - What You Need To Know About Business Corruption
Government/Business/Politics
https://www.createspace.com/Preview/1134206
$2.99/$5.49   70 pages

HOW WE LEARN, WHY WE DON'T - Getting To Know Ourselves
https://www.createspace.com/Preview/1134212
$3.99/$5.99   86 pages

INCONVENIENT REALITY - How Big Business Shoots Us In The Foot, & How Congress And The Press Helped Get Us Into This Mess
https://www.createspace.com/Preview/1134213
Government/Business/Politics
$5.99/$8.99   190 pages

INVADING YOUR PRIVACY - What You Don't Know And What You Should Know
Government/Business/Politics
$1.49   18 pages

LAW IS FOR LAWYERS - The People That We Rely On For Our Protection Can Be The Biggest Offenders Of It
Government/Business/Politics
$1.99   22 pages

ONE POT CLASSICS - The Comfort Food & Easy Clean-up Cookbook
Cookbook
https://www.createspace.com/Preview/1134289
$6.99/$11.49   306 pages

PATHETIC POLITICS & PERFORMANCE - What We Should Know About Our System Of Government
Government/Business/Politics
https://www.createspace.com/Preview/1134290
$4.99/6.99   112 pages

POWER BREEDS ABUSE - Or To Put This Another Way… On Some Level, Power Always Leads To Corruption
Government/Business/Politics
https://www.createspace.com/Preview/1134291
$2.99/4.99   48pages

SELECTING A CONTRACTOR - Making The Right Choice The First Time
Construction
$1.49   11 pages

SELLING & STAGING A HOME - Getting The Most From Your Efforts
Construction
$1.49   6 pages

SENIOR FRIENDLY HOME DESIGN - Making A House Safe

Construction
$1.49   11 pages

SOCIAL NETWORKING - The Downside To Exposing
Yourself
Human Nature
$1.49   5 pages

THE PRESS'S ROLE IN BAD POLITICS - What They Do, And
How They Contribute
Government/Business/Politics
https://www.createspace.com/Preview/1134295
$1.99/$5.49   32 pages

THE WAR ON DRUGS - How It Harms Everyone
Government/Business/Politics
$1.49   6 pages

TO SELL OR REMODEL - Making The Right Decision
Construction
$1.99   9 pages

TRAVEL DEALS & BARGINS – Gaming The System To Win
Travel
$1.49   14pages